JACQUES LIPCHITZ: SKETCHES IN BRONZE

ACKNOWLEDGMENT

The publishers wish to acknowledge their gratitude to Paul von Ringelheim, who conceived this book and who has been helpful at every stage of its progress.

JACQUES LIPCHITZ: SKETCHES IN BRONZE

Text: H. H. ARNASON

Photographs of the Maquettes: JAMES MOORE

Consulting Designer: BOB CATO

FREDERICK A. PRAEGER, PUBLISHERS

New York • Washington • London

FREDERICK A. PRAEGER, *Publishers*
111 Fourth Avenue, New York, N.Y. 10003, U.S.A.
5, Cromwell Place, London S.W. 7, England

Published in the United States of America in 1969
by Frederick A. Praeger, Publishers

© 1969 by Frederick A. Praeger, Inc., *Publishers*

All rights reserved

Library of Congress Catalog Card Number: 75-83347

Printed in the United States of America

Photographs on pages 192 to 195: Adolph Studley

Table of Contents

Foreword

It is a tradition in France that sculptors start their statues with a series of maquettes,* or *bozzetti* as Italians have called them. In fact it is still the custom in French art schools to have as a weekly exercise projects on a given theme for which the students must execute a maquette or sketch. These sketches are discussed and judged by the professors in order that the students may learn discipline and composition. It is in this way we have maintained the tradition of the maquette until today.

The nineteenth century was a very fertile period in France in this area: Géricault, Rude, Barye, Carpeaux, Dalou, Daumier, Degas, Rodin and so many others have enriched this field with sketches of great freshness and fascination. The sketches are the first splash, the prime of inspiration which keeps all the spontaneous warmth.

My way of working did not escape this custom either. Throughout my life I have tried to preserve in these clay maquettes the ideas that have come to me spontaneously. Life in our generation is—*hélas*—very chaotic, so in my wanderings a great deal of my possessions have gotten lost or destroyed, especially fragile clay ones.

Some time ago I took account of the maquettes that I had created over the past fifty years and was happy to discover that despite the many trials in my existence a great number of sketches were preserved. I would estimate that fifty to seventy-five works were lost or destroyed. In order to preserve the remaining maquettes for those who might wish to see my first inspirations and encounters, I have now cast these sketches into bronze and have given my consent to make them public to all in this book.

Although the earliest date that we record here is 1914, I remember at least two which must exist with old school friends which were created in 1910 and represent a biblical scene "Ruth and Boaz" and another representing "Perseus and Andromeda." Despite all my efforts to find these friends or their heirs I did not succeed.

I am very happy to present to you these bronzes and have to confess that I myself am waiting to see this assemblage with great impatience and curiosity. For you see it is the first time in my life that the work is all together and presented chronologically showing the total stream of my thoughts, ideas, and encounters. It is my hope that they will give me new elements to acquire a little bit more freedom in the illumination of my art.

J. LIPCHITZ
Hastings-on-Hudson

*Clay sketch or study.

JACQUES LIPCHITZ

by H. H. Arnason

The concept of the sculpture sketch, the maquette, or *bozzetto,* is almost as old as the history of sculpture itself. It is natural that any sculptor, particularly if he is working within the frame of a subject, should make preliminary notations in terms of drawings and, since he is working with three dimensional mass and space, in terms of quick clay or wax models. It is only in the twentieth century that the preliminary sketch has been abandoned by many sculptors, in their obsession for direct and immediate expression in the final work. Jacques Lipchitz, however, was trained at the Académie Julian and Ecole des Beaux-Arts in Paris in a tradition that went back to the origins of French art schools in the seventeenth century. From the beginning, he was taught by his master in sculpture, Raoul Verlet, to fix an idea immediately in clay; and this he has continued to do during the fifty years of his career. In the process, Verlet also constantly quoted the sculptor Rude to the effect that "Sculpture is plates and chestnuts." This quotation baffled Lipchitz, although, respecting Rude as a great sculptor, he was sure that it had a meaning. Finally he realized that Rude was stating the elementary but profound truth that sculpture is flatness and roundness, planes and volumes. With this realization came the further realization that the sketch must not only record the idea, the outlines of the subject, but must also constantly explore fundamental forms and relationships.

The sketches of Lipchitz' student days have long since disappeared, as have most of those made after he first set up his own studio in 1911.* In 1915, during an emotional crisis, he destroyed many of his early works. After his flight to the United States in 1941, more than fifty works, including many sketches, disappeared from his Paris studio and quantities of sketches were destroyed along with major works in 1952 when his New York studio was gutted by fire. However, more than one hundred and fifty of the sketches remain, and through these it is possible to trace the development of Lipchitz' sculpture from 1914 to the present day. It is possible to trace this development perhaps even more accurately and intimately than through the final sculptures, since in these sketches we can see the first suggestion of an idea. We can see the relations between final solutions, the manner in which one idea might be translated into another, entirely different, the manner in which a suggestion noted in the 1920's might be set aside, then revived and transformed in a monumental work of the 1940's.

The original sketches are characteristically in terra cotta, modelled in clay and then

---

*Note: Lipchitz believes two maquettes, *Ruth and Boaz* and *Perseus and Andromeda,* dated 1910, may still exist. See his Foreword. A 1912 *Head of a Woman* (fig. A) was discovered recently too late for inclusion in the catalogue of maquettes.

fired. They are almost without exception first ideas which Lipchitz hoped might be developed into major sculptures. Some of them have been so developed and others not, but Lipchitz differentiates carefully between these sketches, which have the germ of a larger idea, and other small works which he has created from time to time, which were always intended to remain at their original scale. The "transparents" of 1925 and the years following, modelled in wax and then cast in bronze, were such small sculptures in which the artist was experimenting with open space structures. It was never intended that they should be enlarged, although some of them obviously incorporated experiments which later were used in other contexts. In the same manner, a whole series of variations on a chisel, of the early 1950's, and interpretations of found objects, of the later 1950's, were their own justification and were not intended for enlargement. These also were modelled in wax and cast as finished works at their reduced scale. They were never thought of as sketches and are not included in the catalogue of maquettes. Most of the maquettes have remained in terra cotta until recently when, in order to insure their preservation, Lipchitz has cast them in bronze. Simultaneously he has made another cast in plaster, intended for a proposed Lipchitz museum. They thus exist now in three versions: terra cotta, bronze and plaster.

1912-1920

An early surviving maquette is a cubist *Head* of 1914 (1). Before this date Lipchitz had passed from the academic classicism of his student days to a number of experiments in simplification and stylization in which some suggestion of cubist geometry was used in a rather tentative manner. The *Head*, which was made shortly before Lipchitz' visit to Spain in 1914, is almost identical with that of *Woman with Braids*, 1914. It is related to the *Sailor with Guitar* of 1914 (fig. 1), the most completely realized of Lipchitz' first cubist sculptures. Both these figure pieces were made in Spain, which Lipchitz visited together with Diego Rivera and other friends during the summer of 1914. He was caught there by the outbreak of World War I and it was some six months before he was able to return to France. The *Head* belongs to what Lipchitz calls his period of "naïve cubism," being basically a geometric simplification of forms. However, the simplification is that of related sculptural masses rather than of facial anatomy. In this sense, it is well on its way to abstraction.

The next stage in the exploration of cubism is to be seen in a large *Head*, 1915 (fig. 2), in which the features are subordinated to the point of almost complete abstraction. In this, a large, rectangular mass is intersected by a central diagonal ridge which rises into two curving, opposed, horizontal shelves which suggest eye, eyebrow, and ear. The whole is, however, essentially a structure of interpenetrating lines and masses which constitute one of the first completely successful cubist sculptures.

Between 1915 and 1917, Lipchitz, in his stone carvings and his wood constructions, attained his highest degree of abstract simplification. There was always present an implicit figure but this had now been reduced to a series of vertical and horizontal planes penetrating one another, with some counterpoint of curvilinear contours. Symptomatic of this phase is the *Figure*, 1915 (2), which is of a scale and a degree of finish that it might be considered more than a sketch. However, the artist did form this in terra cotta as an idea for a large sculpture, and for this reason it is more massive than most of the stone and wood sculptures of the same period.

Despite the classic beauty of the 1916-17 sculptures, Lipchitz was not content with either their abstraction or their rectangular regularity, so in 1917 he began to complicate the figures and at the same time to introduce a greater degree of mass. From 1917 through the early 1920's the sculptures, both freestanding and relief, involve a complex of curvilinear and diagonal relationships to attain qualities both of richness and monumentality. The figure as a subject assumes a greater presence and frequently begins to take on a specific mood or personality. During this same period Lipchitz also experimented with polychrome relief.

1921

No maquettes survive between 1915 and 1920. In 1921, a number of new experiments and projects emerged. A small *Seated Woman in Armchair* (3) recorded the artist's sense of the curved form of the chair encompassing the rectangular mass of the seated figure. A slightly surrealist quality is introduced by the eyes which are part of the chair form. Thus, the figure of *Seated Woman in Armchair* becomes in a sense a "woman-chair." This small sketch illustrates some of the characteristics of a first idea, since it is realized only from a single view. If it had been developed, Lipchitz would undoubtedly have completed the form in the round.

A tiny *Repentant Magdalene* (4) is merely an asymmetrical, pyramidal form intersected by a curving mass. Despite its extreme simplification, the sense of subject, a reclining figure with a book, is very strong, and in this case it has an effective total spatial realization.

The most interesting project of 1921, although it unfortunately was never realized, was a sculptural group for the garden of a house in Paris. The group consisted of two elements, a horizontal *Reclining Woman* (5-6) and a vertical *Study for Garden Statue* (7), in which a column consisting of a series of penetrated diamond shapes was surmounted by a figure group. The two were to be seen in a vista of forest at the end of an alley of grass. The location in some degree determined the shapes to be used as well as their relationship to one another. The reclining woman is an extremely free, flowing, curvilinear form that marks one of the first complete reactions of the artist against cubism of the more rigidly geometric tradition. The curvilinear form was the result of a commission for a pair of andirons which a friend of the artist's asked him to make for a Louis XV fireplace. The forms of the fireplace forced him totally to abandon his rigid geometry and henceforth curving motifs appeared regularly in his sculpture. The column is of extreme importance as the first idea for a series of vertical, totemistic sculptures which culminate in the great *Figure* of 1930 (fig. 3).

1922-1924

A *Study for Garden Vase*, 1923 (8), is perhaps related in concept to the *Study for Garden Statue*. It is a momentary return to an almost literal representation of an architectural vase from which emerge freely naturalistic plant shapes, a re-examination of

Figure A
HEAD OF A WOMAN
1912, bronze, height 5¹/₂ inches
Collection of the Artist, Hastings-on-Hudson

Figure 2
HEAD
1915, bronze, height 24¹/₂ inches
From the Joseph H. Hirshhorn Collection, New York

Figure 1
SAILOR WITH GUITAR
1914, bronze, height 30 inches
Courtesy Philadelphia Museum of Art

Figure 3
FIGURE
1926-30, bronze, height 85¹/₂ inches
Collection of the artist, Hastings-on-Hudson

Figure 4
BATHER
1923-25, bronze, height 79 inches
Collection of the Artist, Hastings-on-Hudson
(photograph courtesy The Museum of Modern Art)

Figure 5
LA JOIE DE VIVRE
1927, bronze, height 89¹/₄ inches
Collection La Vicomtesse de Noailles, Hyères

natural forms, expressed with the freedom of organic life. Actually this sketch was for a stone flower vase designed for the Barnes Foundation and Lipchitz included the plant shapes in the maquette to show how they would appear. The vase in the Barnes Foundation is now in fact used as a base for a piece of Lipchitz' sculpture.

The sketches between 1922 and 1924 principally take the forms of relief plaques (9-15). In 1922, Albert C. Barnes commissioned the artist to make some bas-reliefs for the newly completed building of the Barnes Foundation (10). The wall space to be filled was an awkward and rather ugly shape and Lipchitz at first was reluctant to attempt the project. However, he finally solved it by creating a powerful diamond form within the frame, flanked with large circular elements in high relief which, together with the deeply undercut pattern, enabled the plaque effectively to subordinate the space within which it was placed. Two other reliefs for Barnes in the forms of lunettes, *Figures with Musical Instruments*, 1923 (11-12), also in very high relief, treat the subjects with great freedom of movement. Although the essential structure of these lunettes is still that of curvilinear cubism, they further document the artist's feeling in the early 1920's that he wished to escape the constrictions of literal cubism.

Cubism for Lipchitz had been the liberating factor, and between 1915 and 1925 he created many of the most important cubist sculptures in existence. He had early realized that cubism had as significant a role to play for sculpture as it did for painting. It was a means of re-examining the nature of sculpture as an art of three dimensional space, mass, plane, and line. It was a means of stating the nature of sculptural form in its simple essence and asserting the work of sculpture as an identity in itself rather than as an imitation of anything else. He feels today that cubist sculpture, by the very three dimensional nature of the sculpture medium, contributed importantly to the cubist definition of space in painting. The cubist sense of form has remained with Lipchitz throughout his life, even though his style has departed radically from that of cubism. When asked when he ceased being a cubist, he invariably answers, "Never!" During the 1920's he achieved some of his most monumental cubist works, such as the *Bather*, 1923-25 (fig. 4) and *La Joie de Vivre, 1927* (fig. 5). Most of the great works of the 1930's maintain the flattened planes and a sense of rectangular masses which derive ultimately from cubism.

However, by 1925 and in a few works even before this date, the desire for liberation from cubist forms became particularly evident in the maquettes. There also became most evident during the early 1920's the desire to find a new content, a new expression. Abstract form for Lipchitz was not enough.

1925

1925 saw in the maquettes a wide variety of experiment. A plaque of *Figure with Guitar* (16) and three small sculptures, two entitled *Woman with Guitar* (17-18) and one *Woman with Mandolin* (19), represent a fascinating series of variations on a theme. The plaque is close to others created between 1922 and 1924. However, the first *Woman with Guitar* (17) composes the figure and the musical instrument in a massive and simplified pyramid which forecasts some of the monumental figures of the 1930's. The second *Woman with Guitar* (18) dissolves both the figure and the guitar, opens up the torso into a negative space and creates an integrated form of "woman-guitar." In *Woman with*

Mandolin (19) the forms are dissolved and integrated even further. The pyramidal space of the previous work is now developed into a tent-like canopy form, and the entire structure takes on a macabre, surrealist quality.

Two other sketches of 1925 mark the first germs of a series of ideas which were to be realized in a number of different major works of the late 1920's and 1930's. These are a figure entitled *Meditation* (20) and another *Man Leaning on His Elbows* (21). *Meditation* is a figure, head on hand, consisting essentially of a single spiral shape given a blocky massiveness through its flattened planes. Space substantially interpenetrates the figure. The other figure, *Man Leaning on His Elbows*, involves a thin and delicate arrangement of arms, attenuated torso and legs in which the solids seem to be serving as frames for the voids. This was now the moment when Lipchitz began to create his transparents in which he reversed solid and void in a series of experiments which were to have the greatest impact on the later history of modern sculpture. The *Meditation* was quickly translated without significant change into larger versions of marble and bronze, and in its general forms served as the basis for such sculptures as the *Reclining Nude with Guitar*, 1928 (fig. 6). In its blocky yet curving masses, it again anticipated aspects of many major works of the 1930's.

Both of these sketches involved an attempt on the part of Lipchitz to create a kind of *Thinker* of his own—after Rodin. The fact that at this period he should be in some degree turning to Rodin is itself of interest. Like many of the experimental sculptors who grew up in the early years of the century, Lipchitz had felt that Rodin was the overpowering influence to be combatted. When, once in his youth, he learned that Rodin had praised one of his works at an exhibition, he was literally sick with anxiety, wondering what could be wrong with his sculpture that Rodin should like it. However, now in the 1920's, at the moment when cubism was no longer enough, he began to realize that Rodin was after all the father of modern sculpture, the master of them all.

The *Man Leaning on His Elbows*, modest though it is in scale and concept, cursory in execution, is a foreshadowing of many of Lipchitz' greatest works. Another startling premonition of his later directions is to be seen in a small sketch of a sacrifice entitled, obviously much later, *First Idea for Sacrifice* (22). This shows a figure holding high a sacrificial cock. It is treated with the utmost immediacy and expressive boldness in the modelling, and fully illustrates Lipchitz' realization at this time that a confidence in his eye and hand must now replace the discipline of cubist blueprints. This figure anticipates the *Sacrifice III*, 1948 (fig. 7), and even more, in its extreme freedom of execution, *Prayer*, 1943 (fig. 8). In both of these later works there is also a fascinating detail of similarity with the *Woman with Mandolin* (19). The priests in both cases are hooded in a manner astonishingly reminiscent of the hooded form in the *Woman with Mandolin*.*

1926

Lipchitz spent the summer of 1926 at Ploumanach, a summer resort on the Brittany coast. There he was intrigued by certain natural formations of rocks in the water off the shore. A series of tremendous stones was suspended on other stones which had been largely washed away by the waves. The large stones were thus held in a delicate equilibrium. When a wind was blowing, they moved and swayed. The feeling of these

---

*Note: The constant interplay of Lipchitz' subjects is evident also in the relationship between the *Sacrifices* and the various versions of *Prometheus and the Vulture*. The gesture of the priest in the *First Idea for Sacrifice* holding the cock with both hands high above his head may also, consciously or unconsciously, have suggested the gesture of the *Return of the Child*, 1941-43.

Figure 6
RECLINING NUDE WITH GUITAR
1928, bronze, length 27 inches
From the Joseph H. Hirshhorn Collection, New York

Figure 7
SACRIFICE III
1948 (cast 1957), bronze, height 49¹/₄ inches
Collection Ted Weiner, Fort Worth

12

Figure 8
PRAYER
1943, bronze, height 42½ inches
Collection R. Sturgis Ingersoll, Penllyn

Figure 9
MOTHER AND CHILD
1929-30, bronze, height 51¼ inches
Collection of the Artist, Hastings-on-Hudson
(photograph courtesy The Museum of Modern Art)

13

great, suspended rocks was captured in a sketch entitled *Ploumanach* (23), which the same year was translated into a finished sculpture. The rock form, an ovoid, rectangular mass with rounded corners has on the face of it a reclining figure suggested by the bathers on the beach. It is suspended over an arch. *Ploumanach* is a massive form but is essentially frontalized with two major views—front and back. This quality of frontality, obviously reminiscent of the powerful confrontations of primitive or archaic art, intrigued Lipchitz at this moment, and he experimented with it in a number of different sculptures. In another small study based on the rocks (24) he suspends three frontalized shapes, one on top of the other: an open circular shape, above this an open diamond, and on top a larger, closed lozenge. All three are placed on a vertical base which is divided into a pair of legs, making of the whole a figure. Although at the time the artist was not particularly (25) even more impressive in its frontalized, primitive power. In this work, a series of heavy, curved or arched shapes intersect at right angles and bear on the top an ovoid head, on the face of which the bather still appears. As the result of a commission, Lipchitz was enabled in 1930 to develop this figure study into the monumental *Figure* of that year (fig. 3), a work which, while it shows no specific influence from any primitive culture, nevertheless has the tremendous power of some great primitive totem. Lipchitz, incidentally, tends to deprecate the supposed influence of African primitive art on cubism. He feels that the influence was essentially a superficial one having to do with appearance conscious of the fact, this figure, related to the rock formations which he had observed, was also a development of the 1921 *Study for Garden Statue*, with its superimposed diamond shapes.

Out of the *Ploumanach* studies of 1926 grew another and different sort of *Figure* rather than with any fundamental forms.

Two other sketches of 1926, *Meditation* (26) and *Standing Figure* (27), reveal further explorations into free organic organizations. *Meditation* is a development of the *Thinker* theme with the figure seated, one arm across his legs and the other arm supporting his head. This is different from the earlier version entitled *Man Leaning on His Elbows* in that the forms are now massively modelled but in an organic rather than in a geometric sense. There is a strong statement of the bony structure of the figure, of massive arms and legs arranged in curving forms which suggest for the first time some of the monumental organic sculptures of the latter 1930's and early 1940's. *Standing Figure* (27) is once more a startling new departure, more freely handled than almost any work by Lipchitz up to this point. In this maquette the clay is pulled and twisted in a quite literally baroque manner. A sense of movement, of floating draperies, is apparent. Here begins a new vein of exploration which is to be pursued in the sketches of the next few years and in many of the major sculptures of the 1940's and 1950's.

1928

Most of Lipchitz' sculpture from the time he turned to cubism up to this point (with the notable exception of the 1925 and subsequent "transparents") had been organized within the invisible block. Space frequently interpenetrated this block, but there was a limited emphasis placed on the statement of the external spatial existence of the block, or movement within surrounding space in the manner of Late Renaissance or

Baroque sculpture. The *Standing Figure* of 1926 was an exploration of the problems of three-dimensional spatial existence, utilizing the twist of the figure in order to suggest movement and existence in surrounding space. This particular problem, which he had last explored in his proto-cubist sculptures in 1913-14, now began again to become of more importance to Lipchitz.

A *Reclining Figure* (28), massive and rocklike in its formation, uses a form of Renaissance contrapposto in order to emphasize spatial existence. Two reliefs, *Dancer with Veil* (29) and *Reclining Woman with Drapery* (30), are arabesques of curvilinear movement across the surface of the plane. In these works, particularly the latter, the interest in movement results in a considerable utilization of line. Finally, in the sketch, *Dancer with Veil* (31), there is a full realization of baroque spatial movement. This is a flying figure moving to the left with the veils floating out behind her to the right. The figure is interpenetrated with several openings and is composed in a great spiral twist in the grand manner of Baroque sculpture. The looseness and freeness of the clay modelling emphasize the qualities of motion which the artist is seeking. They also emphasize an emotional content which is once more a remarkable anticipation of some of the most profound expressions of the later sculptures. This figure with its running, twisting movement, is the first statement of an organization to be used in numerous major sculptures, such as the *Prometheus* and the *Pegasus* series.

1929

The exploration of the new and expanded spatial concept continued in a relief *Couple in Hammock* (35) and *Reclining Figure* (36). These are intriguing, not only in the extreme interpenetration of the solids with voids which take on their own shape identity, but also in that the figures develop further the bone-like quality noted in the *Meditation* of 1926. They are curious anticipations of the so-called bone sculptures of Henry Moore.

A series of variations on a theme, a *Standing Figure* (37) and *Woman Leaning on a Column* (38-40), as well as *Reclining Woman on a Puff* (41), all seem to embody some explorations of formal problems in terms of free expression. The first of these, *Standing Figure*, is a rather direct sketch of a figure leaning on a post or column with a twisting pose reminiscent again of Renaissance contrapposto. The other three versions of *Woman Leaning on a Column* and the *Reclining Woman on a Puff* are macabre figures with strong surrealist overtones. For Lipchitz they obviously represented not only certain technical and formal experiments with the medium of clay, pushing it to the limits of distortion, but also the exploration of a new kind of subject matter, one of free fantasy. A final work of 1929, a tiny *Dancer* (42), is an unusually lively experiment in a rotating shape, a flying circular veil spinning around an axis.

During this entire process of re-examining and expanding his formal vocabulary, Lipchitz was also intensely involved in the achievement of a new content in his work, a new expressive means. 1928 had been a year of tragedy for him. He lost his father, and his beloved sister died at almost the same time. Something of his sorrow is evident in the *Mother and Child* (43). The crouching mother clasps the child tightly to her breast and lifts her head in a shriek of anguish. The Mother and Child theme continued to haunt the artist for many years, and as it was realized in magnificent works of the 1930's and

1940's, it meant many different things to him. At times, the child is Lipchitz himself; at times it is his sculpture threatened with total destruction. The Mother and Child can symbolize the agony of war and at another moment the exultation of escape and peace. A curious assimilation of motifs resulted from a bird-like shape which Lipchitz saw in a cloud in 1929 and quickly recorded (44). This shape in his mind became identified with the Mother and Child idea and was used in the great version of 1930 (fig. 9).

The artist's sufferings during this year, his consciousness of the imminence of death, led him to the fundamental themes of birth and the creation of life. In the *Encounter* (45) two standing figures seem to be in the midst of a struggle which is also an embrace. This is the first idea for such a work as *Jacob and the Angel* of 1932 (fig. 10). *The Couple* (46) is an embrace, which to Lipchitz became a supreme symbol of the very act of life and procreation. In one of his first essays in classical mythology, the artist in 1929 portrayed a *Leda and the Swan* (47) in a highly direct and literal manner. This is a freely-modelled group with broken outlines of the wings of the bird. The stylized curving legs of the recumbent Leda are utilized in much the same form in the monumental sculpture of *The Couple* (fig. 11), also known as *The Cry*, which was first designed in 1929. This latter embracing group, incidentally, combines in a disturbing effect the shrieking head of the *Mother and Child* from the sketch of the same year.

1930

The maquettes of the Embrace motif pleased Lipchitz and, as a slight diversion, he made a curious little *Man with a Clarinet*, 1929 (48). The man and the clarinet are composed in a single sweeping S-curve. Although he returned to this theme again in 1931 (63), the first version did not particularly satisfy him. He began then to experiment with a more significant subject, the *Return of the Prodigal Son*, and during 1930 he made at least three variant sketches (49-51). In these the figure of the prodigal arches over that of the mother, and kisses her with the passionate thirst of the traveller returned to the wells of his homeland. The two figures are blocked out in undulating masses which encompass a large central void. The *Return of the Prodigal Son* was transformed into a finished sculpture in 1931 (fig. 12), one of the massive and violently expressive groups of the early 1930's. It is also one of the earliest major representations of the themes of departure and reunion which haunted Lipchitz during the period of Nazi dominance and its culmination in World War II. A curious aspect of the sketches for the *Return of the Prodigal Son* is that the organization of the figures actually derives from the 1929 *Man with a Clarinet*, although Lipchitz was not aware of this fact until the coincidence suddenly struck him many years later.

In 1930 there were a number of other experiments. The *Figure* of 1926 (25) was reworked in a form essentially that of the final sculpture with eyes in the head replacing the bathers (52). Two versions of a *Seated Woman* (53-54) carried on the spatial experiments of the transparents and of the 1925 *Man Leaning on His Elbows*. These figures take on a more geometric order in the curving blocks of arms and legs, indicating that the artist was perhaps thinking rather specifically of their translation into a larger sculpture, a translation which, however, was never realized in quite this form.

There was another essay at the theme of the kneeling mother clutching her child, with her head broken apart in a screaming cry (55). A number of strange amorphic forms (56-58) seem to be based on studies of rock formations; and a monstrous beast entitled *Mishugas* (59) reflected a period of rage and disgust which the artist does not now care to recall.

1931

A theme which Lipchitz turned to again and again between 1930 and 1933 was the bust of a woman, generally leaning on her elbows. He explored this subject in innumerable variations, in terra cotta sketches, in wax and bronze transparents, in finished works in bronze or marble. It was obviously a theme with a considerable personal significance, but just as obviously the explorations have the character of tasks which he had set himself, to discover new sculptural possibilities through the playing of variations on a single theme (1930: 60-61; 1931: 62-63).

In 1931, the artist continued with the subjects of the contending figures. In *The Fight* (65) there is a relatively representational statement of a victor crouched over his recumbent enemy. More significant are two versions of *Jacob and the Angel* (66-67). Although in his early years Lipchitz had not been a devout believer, he had begun, during the 1920's, to read the Bible intensively and to think continually about the meaning of the stories told therein. He was particularly puzzled by the story of Jacob and the Angel in which the Angel is sent by God and, as Lipchitz interprets it, is a manifestation of God Himself. What, Lipchitz asked himself, could be the significance of this story in which God challenges the man to battle and then rewards him for his courage? To Lipchitz the key lay in the word "courage" and it was this quality in man that God was praising. The sketches of *Jacob and the Angel* are extremely free, floating and combatting forms, with space moving through and around them. They represent a further exploration of sculptural problems of space and movement, as well as the statement of a profound theme. While maintaining something of the flying quality of the sketches, the final sculpture of 1932 is much more massive and compacted. Again the battle seems to become an embrace of love.

In 1931, Lipchitz also produced the first tentative sketch for a *Prometheus* (68), a reclining figure, his back arched in suffering. Actually this sketch was named only recently and it has little or no relationship to the tremendous realizations of *Prometheus Strangling the Vulture*, produced between 1936 and 1944. That theme really had its origin in the 1933 sketch (96).

In the 1931 *Study for "Song of the Vowels"* (69), with its harp-like shape mounted on a pillar, final form is given to another motif which had delighted the artist for several years. Enchanted by the sound of harps which he had heard at the Salle Pleyel in 1928, Lipchitz in that same year began creating in his transparents in a number of harp shapes. He also made harp structures in bronze and stone and in 1931-32 he gave monumental form to the theme in a ten-foot high *Song of the Vowels* created for a garden at Le Pradet, France (fig. 13).*

1932

Variations on the head, hair and arms of a woman continued to appear during 1932 (70-78) and 1933 (83-87). In some of these the floating hair becomes remarkably similar

---

*Note: Now at the Kunsthaus, Zürich.

Figure 10
JACOB AND THE ANGEL
1932, bronze, length 47¹/₂ inches
Collection of the Artist, Hastings-on-Hudson
(photograph courtesy The Museum of Modern Art)

Figure 11
THE COUPLE
1929, bronze, length 58 inches

Figure 12
RETURN OF THE PRODIGAL SON
1931, bronze, height 44 inches
Collection of the Artist, Hastings-on-Hudson

Figure 13
SONG OF THE VOWELS
1931-32, bronze, height 80 inches

Figure 14
PROMETHEUS WITH VULTURE
1936, bronze, height 16¹/₂ inches

to the wings of the angel-like form which Lipchitz had seen in a cloud formation in 1929, and which was for him inextricably involved with the Mother and Child theme. Many of these studies were explorations of interior or negative sculptural space, and the interest in this problem perhaps led the artist in 1932 to a series of studies of helmet or skull heads (79-80) in which the interior space is open and enveloped by a skin or bone structure, pierced with great eye holes. Again one is reminded of Henry Moore's helmet heads of the 1940's and 1950's.

Another scene of terrible conflict was suggested to Lipchitz when his friend, the poet Juan Larrea, returned from Peru. In Peru, according to Larrea, at certain fiestas a condor is caught, its feet are literally sewn to the hide of a bull and the two are then freed in an arena. There results a fantastic and horrible battle until one or both are killed. The story moved Lipchitz deeply. At the moment when Hitler and the Nazis were coming into power in Germany, the artist was entering upon a period of profound depression, and he felt that the bull and the condor signified the insane brutality of the world. The two surviving sketches of 1932 (81-82) are modelled with a passion, a furious energy which reflects the emotions of the artist in the face of this frightening conflict. The clay is scarred, undercut and torn like the bodies of the fighters. The jagged textures and contours emphasize further the violence of the scene. This is a work which once more looks forward to the most freely expressive sculptures of the 1940's and 1950's. In those the bull, appearing here in Lipchitz' sculpture for the first time, as a symbol of suffering, continues to reappear in his sculpture in many different contexts.

1933

In 1933, Lipchitz returned again to the theme of bull and condor, this time in the form of a relief (88). 1933 was the year Hitler actually came to power and the artist was terrified by a sense of insanity let forth on the world. He felt passionately the need to express his fears and his resistance in his sculpture. An obsession overcame him of Hitler as the murderer, not only of mankind but of all art, and the image of his sculpture in danger of total destruction came forth in a series of sketches on themes of rescue (*Rescue of the Child*, 89-91). The first of these (89) adapts the motif of the upstretched arms—in this case the mother's arms holding the child up, away from danger—on which he had played so many variants during the past three years. In the second (90) the child, with outstretched arms, is held high above the head of the mother in a gesture similar to the way the cock had been held in the arms of the priest in the *First Idea for Sacrifice* of 1925. This work is loosely and freely modelled, the mother and child rise like an undulating column from the base of a crouching figure. The third version (91) is the most complex in organization. The mother, still holding the child high, strives to escape from great, attacking serpents, while the father struggles vainly to free them from the serpents.

Other sculptures of 1933 reflected the artist's alternating moods of despair, hatred and hope. Three maquettes of embracing couples, *The Embrace* (92-93) and *The Rape* (94), assume a deadly violence in which love and hate are interchanged, although the idea of the embrace as a symbol of procreation and a hope of new life always remains in the artist's mind.

The Strangulation (95) is a strange summation of these battles of love or death. The figures are grouped in a manner almost identical with those in the *Return of the Prodigal Son* of 1930-31. The uppermost figure in this sketch clutches the throat of the victim but at the same time seems in the act of a passionate kiss. The theme of Prometheus appears in a developed form (96). Here it is a triumphant Prometheus, symbol of the victory of light over darkness, in process of destroying the vulture. This group draws close to the final version, in the powerful, twisting movement of the figures in space. In fact, as is so frequently the case with these sketches, it perhaps goes beyond the finished sculpture in the dynamic interplay of solids, space and motion.

The hatred and fear of Fascism began to find a specific outlet in a project for a tremendous monument of *David and Goliath*. In the first of four remaining sketches dated 1933 (97-100), David stands over a recumbent Goliath, twisting a cord about his neck. In the subsequent sketches the figures are reversed, with the huge Goliath rising up vertically and David pulling back with all his strength on the great cable cord which he has twisted around the throat of the giant. The final sketch, placing the figures on a column, reduces the size of the giant to a more human scale. The two figures straining mightily against one another establish a terrific state of tension which might have become melodramatic were it not for the intensity of conviction apparent in the sculpture. The project was executed on a larger scale and the plaster was exhibited in 1934 at the Salon des Surindépendents. Lipchitz wished there to be no doubt about his intent, so he placed a swastika on the chest of Goliath. The statue caused him considerable difficulty with German agents, who in the guise of art critics began to show intense interest in visiting and examining the artist's studio. However, it remained unharmed in the basement of the Musée National d'Art Moderne during the entire German occupation.

A series of sketches on an entirely unrelated theme seems to have provided some relaxation from the artist's emotional conflicts during this year. These were studies for a portrait of the painter Géricault, whose work Lipchitz has long loved and admired (101-104). Lipchitz, of course, is one of the most brilliant sculpture portraitists of our time and normally his portraits are simply made to life scale from the model. The *Géricault* was modelled after a death mask of the painter and in these small sketches the sculptor is playing variations as he attempts to recreate the personality and the genius of a great artist.

1934

The major sculpture of the 1930's is characterized by a continuing search for a monumental expression. Works created between 1929 and 1935 were usually organized in heavy block forms which achieve a tremendous effect of density and weight. As suggested, a sense of cubist control persisted much longer in the large sculptures than in the sketches. The desire to create a great monument which resulted in the 1933 *David and Goliath*, also dominated the artist's thinking during 1934 and 1935. Most of the surviving sketches of 1934 are studies for such a monument. A series of four, *Toward a New World* (107-110), shows with increasing complications figures carrying a flag and digging in the earth. They are organized in a violently agitated pyramid interpenetrated spatially, with the great flag, in undulating motion, sweeping over and encompassing the group. Even in the small maquettes, the composition expresses a furious energy which is reminiscent of Rude's *Marseillaise* on the Arc de Triomphe. These sketches and three other

Studies for a Monument (111-113) were inspired by a temporary enthusiasm for Soviet Russia, which was perhaps a reaction against the growing power of Fascism. This interest in the Soviet persisted until Lipchitz actually visited Russia in 1935.

1936

No sketches remain from 1935, but 1936 was marked by a number of varied experiments. The sense of fear recurs in *The Terrified One* (117), a strange herma figure which seems to grow out of the many studies of the woman's head and arms. Two *Studies for a Bridge Monument* (118-119) illustrate his continuing desire to make a great architectural sculpture, and it may be that the *Scene of Civil War* (120), inspired by the Spanish Civil War, was also designed in the context of a project for a monument.

The Prometheus theme which had concerned the artist at least since 1933 began to reach its final solution in 1936. In two versions of a *Study of Prometheus* (121-122) Lipchitz, as in the 1933 *Rescue of the Child* (91), went back for inspiration to the ancient sculpture of Laocoön, and posed the figure in a somewhat similar spiral, with the right arm curving up over the head. The ultimate solution, however, was arrived at in a larger bronze study, *Prometheus with Vulture*, 1936 (fig. 14), and Lipchitz finally received a commission for a tremendous plaster which was installed over the portal of the Grand Palais for the 1937 Paris World's Fair. This plaster has since been destroyed, but the Prometheus now exists in a monumental bronze, *Prometheus Strangling the Vulture II*, dating 1944-1953 (fig. 15).

1937-1943

The unsettled years immediately preceding World War II and the first two or three years of the War produced very few maquettes or, for that matter, very few major sculptures. In 1938 there were two sketches for a portrait of Gertrude Stein (123-124). In 1920, Lipchitz had portrayed Gertrude Stein in a massive simplified Buddha head (fig 16). The later sketches are much more human and appealing in their portrayal of the aging and rather weary poet.

In May, 1940, with the German invasion of France, Lipchitz left Paris and settled in Toulouse. In 1941, with the help of his American friends, he was able to reach the United States. The flight and the safe arrival in America are commemorated in two sculptures, *Flight*, 1940 (fig. 17) and *Arrival*, 1941 (fig. 18), and in a maquette, *Study for "Return of the Child,"* 1941 (125), which was also developed in a larger granite version in the same year. Here we have the final realization of the motif which first occurred in the *First Study for Sacrifice* of 1925 and was then given its present context in the 1933 sketches on the theme of *Rescue of the Child*. Whereas these earlier versions emerged from a fear which the artist sought to escape, the 1941 *Return of the Child* is an ecstatic prayer of thanks. In its note of jubilation, it also takes us back to the *Return of the Prodigal Son*.

By 1942, Lipchitz had again begun to establish his pattern of work in his New York studio on Washington Square South. The enthusiasm for his new environment resulted in a period of intense activity in which he produced sculpture involving many new directions and experiments. Three maquettes, *Study for Benediction*, 1942 (126-128), revealed the genesis of the direction he was to follow for his most monumental efforts of the 1940's. At this point he had abandoned the massive, rectangular blocks of the earlier 1940's and was moving towards a more curvilinear organization with an accent on rounded volumes. This same volumetric approach is seen in the final sketch for *Prometheus Strangling the Vulture*, 1943 (129). In the sketch, as in the large sculpture, the curving forms are put into energetic motion, and the broken outlines of the flying drapery and vulture's wings make this one of the most completely baroque sculptures of Lipchitz' career.

1944-45

During the next two years, Lipchitz proceeded with many large projects, two of which, *Birth of the Muses* and *Song of Songs*, revealed, in their use of the arts as a subject, the artist's continually growing optimism in the New World. The *Study for "Birth of the Muses,"* 1944 (131), is a Pegasus form, designed from the beginning to be seen as a relief. The flying horse, with head turned back, is a wonderful complex of deeply undercut shapes of legs, wings and body. The same essential form appeared again in two sketches for *Pegasus*, dated 1949 (145-146), one an actual relief and the other freestanding. It was finally realized as a large wall sculpture, *Birth of the Muses*, 1944-50.

1947

The maquettes of 1947 revealed some further stylistic departures which were soon translated into some of the final sculptures of the late 1940's. Two versions of the *Couple* (133-134) illustrate the new direction. The first (133) is one of those periodic returns of a relatively naturalistic approach with which Lipchitz frequently refreshes his vision. The other (134) is a fantastic grouping of amoeba-like forms which seems to be pursuing some of the ideas of the surrealist bone figures of the 1920's.

Most of the sketches of this year involve such experiments in fantasy, with figures composed in strongly linear arabesques of wildly distorted naturalistic forms. The interest in curving, linear movement is particularly evident in a series of studies for dancers —*Dancer* (135), *Dancer with Veil* (136) and *Study for Dancer with Braids* (137). A sketch for *Hagar* (138) was the same year transformed into the finished sculpture in which the enormously enlarged curving arms and hands of the deserted Hagar comfort the child in her own moment of despair.

1948

The year 1948 was largely taken up with studies for the statue of *Notre Dame de Liesse*, on which he worked for the next several years (140-144). Lipchitz was deeply moved when he, as he said, "a Jew, true to the faith of his ancestors," should have been asked to create a shrine for the Madonna. The problem for him was a difficult one which he attacked with furious energy, making countless sketches and drawings. The solution at which he finally arrived, of the Blessing Madonna, whose form is assimilated to and becomes one with the heart-shaped mandorla which enfolds her, drew on the experience of his entire working life. The organization of interior space surrounded by the solid walls of the mandorla suggests his concern with spatial problems going back to the

Figure 15
PROMETHEUS STRANGLING THE VULTURE II
1944-53, bronze, height 102 inches
Collection Walker Art Center, Minneapolis

Figure 16
GERTRUDE STEIN
1920, bronze, height 13¹/₂ inches
The Detroit Institute of Arts

Figure 17
FLIGHT
1940, bronze, height 14¹/₂ inches

Figure 18
ARRIVAL
1941, bronze, height 21 inches
Collection of the Artist, Hastings-on-Hudson

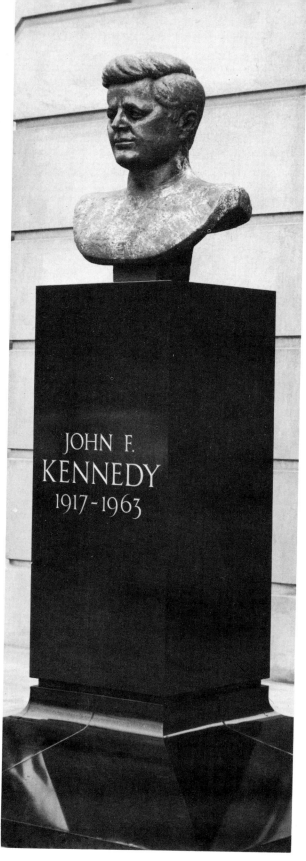

Figure 19
JOHN F. KENNEDY
1965, bronze, height 31 inches
International Students House, London

Figure 20
DANIEL GREYSOLON, SIEUR DU LUTH
1965, bronze, height 108 inches
University of Minnesota, Duluth

transparents of the 1920's. However, the essence of the altarpiece lies in its profound statement of the concept of metamorphosis, a concept which has been central to Lipchitz' sculpture during most of his career as a mature artist. The idea of change or becoming goes like a thread through the sculpture of Lipchitz. In it are involved all the thoughts that the artist has had on birth and life and death. Europa, assimilated to the bull, becomes one with the godhead. Theseus killing the Minotaur seems to be destroying a part of himself. Jacob in his struggle with the Angel absorbs the spirit of God. The Virgin of Mercy, as she is transformed into a mandorla, becomes a symbol of the transformation of the flesh and the spirit.

1949-1959

Relatively few maquettes survive from the 1950s. The tragic fire which destroyed his studio in 1952 resulted in the loss not only of many major sculptures, including the plasticine model of *Notre Dame de Liesse*, but also of a large proportion of the sketches created in the United States. In his new studio at Hastings-on-Hudson, New York, to which he moved in 1953, Lipchitz has, in recent years, been working incessantly on the creation of major sculptures and the casting of many of the works into bronze. Ideas for monumental sculptures continue to come to him.

In 1949, he made sketches for a biblical scene (147-148) whose complex of forms suggest the possibility of monumental treatment. In 1951 he received a commission from the Fairmount Park Association in Philadelphia, which was finally finished in 1958 as a 12-foot high statue of *The Spirit of Enterprise*. Sketches for this were made during 1953 (*Sketch for Enterprise*, 149-151). This work has points of relationship with the final solution for the *Prometheus*, although the conception is that of a triumphant explorer of a new world rather than a battle between light and darkness.

There were occasional portrait studies—*Study for Portrait*, 1956 (152) and *Sketch for Yulla Lipchitz*, 1956 (153)—a delightful interpretation of his second wife. In 1958, Lipchitz worked with the architect, Philip Johnson, on a project of a Roofless Church in New Harmony, Indiana, to house the second cast of *Notre Dame de Liesse*. Lipchitz' contribution was a beautiful gateway (155) which reveals his rarely exploited talent for architectural decoration. In looking at it, one is reminded curiously enough of the very early naturalistic *Study for Garden Vase* which he created in 1923.

After the plasticine model of the *Notre Dame de Liesse* was destroyed in the fire, Lipchitz created a lovely small bronze of a *Virgin in Flames*. Although he did not develop this theme in this form, the image has remained with him and he has recently returned to it in a variety of works. In the early 1940's, the artist, while using great curving volumes for many of his major works, was also continually experimenting with other shapes and techniques. He produced a number of works involving dominant use of line and others in which the clay is torn and twisted on thin, writhing sheets which produce effects of intense emotional conflict. *The Pilgrim* of 1942 and *The Prayer* of 1943 (fig. 8) in which the figures are turned inside out, literally disembowelled before our eyes, are the most terrifying examples of this approach. The handling of the material in these works anticipates to some degree the flame-like contours of the *Virgin in Flames*, and, even more, a 1957 sketch, *Lesson of a Disaster* (154), in which the entire figure is simply one single burning mass. The flame, which is the supreme symbol of metamorphosis and purification, became the basic form and concept in a great *Our Tree of Life* on which the artist is still working (156-157).

1960-

Since 1960 the sculptural activities of Lipchitz have, if anything, increased and accelerated. He has spent every summer since 1962 in Italy, working with foundries on casts of his major sculptures. During this same period he found time to create twenty-six small bronzes in which he permitted his fantasy full play. Twenty-five of these he entitled, as a group, *Images of Italy*. These are not maquettes for larger works, but finished compositions at a reduced scale.

The subject of the Madonna has continued to haunt him, the most recent result being a highly baroque version of the Assumption, *Between Heaven and Earth*, which has been widely exhibited in Europe and the United States.

Portrait subjects of the period include Andre Cournint, Jules Stein, Samuel D. Leidesdorf and Albert Skira. The most important portrait commission was that of President *John F. Kennedy* (fig. 19); variants in London and Newark, New Jersey. This posthumous portrait presented certain difficulties since, in portraiture, the living model is highly essential to Lipchitz. This was solved when Lipchitz found a man with a remarkable resemblance to the late president who agreed to sit for the preliminary modelling of the bust (158). Working from this model, and from innumerable photographs taken from every conceivable angle, the artist produced an impressive, somewhat generalized portrait which nevertheless catches admirably the appearance and forthright personality of President Kennedy.

The other major commission of the early 1960's was again a portrait of a man no longer alive, in this case a man of whose appearance no record exists. This is *Daniel Greysolon, Sieur du Luth* (fig. 20), the seventeenth-century French explorer after whom the city of Duluth, Minnesota, was named. The portrait was a challenge to both the imagination and the strong historical sense of the artist, with the result that he made half a dozen sketches suggesting variations of pose and costume (159). He even made studies from a nude model, the better to capture the underlying anatomy (160). The statue is mounted on a thirteen-foot granite pedestal and is thus characteristically seen from below at an abrupt angle. Lipchitz deliberately distorted the proportions of the figure, exaggerating the upper part and diminishing the legs, in order to correct the optical effect.

Most recently the artist has been working on another of his great mythological themes, that of *Bellerophon Taming Pegasus* (161). This theme again symbolizes the victory of law over chaos, of civilization over barbarism. It relates, thus, to the *Prometheus* concept, although the forms derive from earlier versions of the *Pegasus*. The small but dominant figure of Bellerophon taming the huge and violently agitated Pegasus is also, at a certain remove, reminiscent of the 1933 sketches for *David and Goliath*, which the artist has always wanted to develop into a monument. When finally realized at full scale, the *Bellerophon* will stand forty feet high on its column; it will be one of the artist's most impressive sculptures not only in its scale, but even more so in the wild conflict expressed in its expansive, broken baroque contours.

Today, as he approaches eighty, Jacques Lipchitz continues to work with a vitality and imagination undimmed by time and seemingly in a state of explosive expansion. As he completes one major project or commission after another, he continually finds time for new experiments in the form of maquettes—sketches which contain the first ideas for the great works of the future.

Chronology

1891	Chaim Jacob Lipchitz born August 22 at Druskieniki, Lithuania.
1902-6	Commercial school in Bialystok.
1906-9	High school in Vilna.
1909-10	Arrived in Paris, October, 1909. Became "free pupil" of Jean Antoine Ingalbert at Ecole des Beaux-Arts. Attended sculpture classes of Raoul Verlet at Académie Julian. Also studied drawing, art history and anatomy.
1911	Established studio in Montparnasse.
1913	Met Picasso and other cubists through Diego Rivera.
1914	Visited Majorca with Rivera and other friends. Returned to Paris at end of year. *Sailor with Guitar. Woman with Braids.*
1915	*Head,* and other major cubist sculptures.
1916	Met Juan Gris. Several major stone cubist sculptures, including *Figure, Standing Personage* and *Man with a Guitar.*
1920	First one man exhibition at Léonce Rosenberg Gallery. Maurice Raynal published first monograph on Lipchitz. *Portrait of Gertrude Stein.*
1922	Commission for five bas-reliefs for Barnes Foundation, Merion, Pennsylvania.
1925	Moved to Boulogne-sur-Seine, house designed by Le Corbusier. *Bather.* Began to work on a series of "transparents" through experimentation with "cire perdue" process.
1927	*La Joie de Vivre* for garden of the Vicomtesse de Noailles at Hyères.
1928	*Reclining Nude with Guitar.*
1929	*The Couple.*
1930	First large retrospective exhibition, Galérie de la Renaissance (Jeanne Bucher), Paris. *Figure.* First appearance of *Mother and Child* and *Prodigal Son* motifs.
1931-32	*Return of the Prodigal Son. Song of the Vowels. The Harpists.*
1932	*Jacob and the Angel. Head.*
1933	*Portrait of Géricault. Woman Leaning on Elbows.* Sketches for *David and Goliath.*
1934	Exhibition of plaster of *David and Goliath* at Salon des Surindépendents.
1935	First large exhibition in United States, Brummer Gallery, New York.
1936-37	*Prometheus* executed for Paris World's Fair; awarded gold medal. Room devoted to his sculpture at exhibition held during Fair, "Les Maîtres de l'art indépendant," Petit Palais.
1938	*Rape of Europa.*
1940	Moved to Toulouse. *Flight.*
1941	Moved to New York City. *Arrival. Return of the Child.*
1942	Began to exhibit regularly at Buchholz Gallery (later the Curt Valentin Gallery), New York. *The Pilgrim. Spring. The Promise.*
1943-44	Worked on *Prometheus Strangling the Vulture,* commission for Ministry of Health and Education, Rio de Janeiro, and on *Mother and Child.*

1945	*The Rescue.*
1946	Visited Paris where he exhibited at Galérie Maeght. Was made a Chevalier de la Légion d'Honneur. *Song of Songs.*
1947-48	Settled in Hastings-on-Hudson, New York. Began series of studies for commission for the church of Notre-Dame-de Toute-Grace, at Assy. *Miracle II. Dancer with Braids. Pastorale. Hagar.*
1949	*Mother and Child.*
1950-51	Relief *Birth of the Muses.* Large model of *Notre Dame de Liesse* for Assy.
1952	Fire in New York studio destroyed many sketches and major works. Several commissioned portraits.
1953	Moved into new studio at Hastings-on-Hudson. *Virgin in Flames.*
1954	Retrospective, The Museum of Modern Art, New York; Walker Art Center, Minneapolis; The Cleveland Museum of Art.
1955-56	*Hagar in the Desert.*
1958	Received Honorary Doctorate, Brandeis University. Completed *Spirit of the Enterprise* for Fairmount Park Association, Philadelphia. Worked on gateway for Roofless Church in New Harmony, Indiana, with architect, Philip Johnson, to house second cast of *Notre Dame de Liesse.* Exhibition, Stedelijk Museum, Amsterdam; Rijksmuseum Kröller-Müller, Otterloo; Basel; Dortmund; Paris; Brussels; London.
1959	Series of fantastic bronzes from small objects, which were shown in exhibition "A la limite du possible" at Fine Arts Associates, New York.
1963	Work on *Our Tree of Life.* Large retrospective exhibition at University of California at Los Angeles; San Francisco Museum of Art; Denver Art Museum; Fort Worth Art Center; Walker Art Center; Des Moines Art Center; Philadelphia Museum of Art
1963-65	Exhibition "157 Bronze Sketches, 1912-1962," Otto Gerson Gallery, New York; Currier Gallery; Albright-Knox Art Gallery; Atlanta Art Association; Joslyn Art Museum; Tweed Gallery of the University of Minnesota; The Arts Club of Chicago; Detroit Institute of Arts; also circulated internationally to Buenos Aires; Santiago; Caracas; Lima; Melbourne; Auckland and Wellington.
1964	Exhibition of *Between Heaven and Earth* at Documenta International, Carnegie International. Exhibition of cubist sculpture and reliefs at Phillips Collection.
1965	Award for cultural achievement from Boston University and one man exhibition there. Exhibition at opening of Jerusalem Museum. Installation of *John F. Kennedy* in London and Newark. Exhibition at Newark Museum. Installation of *Daniel Greysolon, Sieur du Luth* in Duluth, Minnesota.
1966	Gold medal from Academy of Arts and Letters and exhibition of works there. Exhibition Makler Gallery, Philadelphia. Exhibitions annually 1964, 1965, 1966 at Marlborough-Gerson Gallery, New York.
1967	Presentation by the artist of bronze *Between Heaven and Earth* to village of Hastings-on-Hudson.
1968-69	Continues work of casting major sculptures in Pietrasanta, Italy. Lipchitz has been working there during the summers since 1963. His major project is at present the completion of *Bellerophon Taming Pegasus.* He also continues casting and finishing bronze sculptures during the rest of the year at the Modern Art Foundry, and Avnet & Shaw Foundry, New York. At present he is working on large and small bronze versions of *Lesson of a Disaster.*
1969	Dedication of monumental sculpture, *Peace on Earth*, Los Angeles County Music Center. Award of Merit from Einstein University. Medal of achievement from American Institute of Architects.

Selected Bibliography

Dermée, Paul. "Lipchitz," *Esprit Nouveau*, Paris, no. 2, November, 1920, pp. 169-182.

Raynal, Maurice. *Lipchitz* (Art d'Aujourd'hui). *Action*, Paris, 1920.

George, Waldemar. "Jacques Lipchitz," *Das Kunstblatt*, Berlin, vol. 6, 1922, pp. 58-64.

"The Technique of Jacques Lipchitz," *Broom*, Paris, vol. 2, 1922, pp. 216-219.

Parkes, Kineton. "The Constructional Sculpture of Jacques Lipchitz," *The Architect*, London, vol. 114, September 18, 1925, pp. 202-204.

Huidobro, Vincente. "Jacques Lipchitz," *Cahiers d'Art*, Paris, vol. 3, 1928, pp. 153-158.

Vitrac, Roger. *Jacques Lipchitz* (Les sculpteurs français nouveaux, 7). Paris, Librairie Gallimard, 1929.

Guéguen, Paul. "Jacques Lipchitz; ou, l'histoire naturelle magique," *Cahiers d'Art*, Paris, vol. 7, 1932, pp. 252-258.

Schwartzberg, Miriam B. *The Sculpture of Jacques Lipchitz*. New York, New York University, 1941. (Typescript of thesis in the library of The Museum of Modern Art, New York.)

Lipchitz, Jacques. "The Story of My Prometheus," *Art in Australia*, Sydney, ser. 4, no. 6, June-August, 1942, pp. 29-35.

Twelve Bronzes by Jacques Lipchitz. New York, Buchholz Gallery, Curt Valentin, 1943.

The Drawings of Jacques Lipchitz. New York, Buchholz Gallery, Curt Valentin, 1944.

Rewald, John. "Jacques Lipchitz's Struggle," *The Museum of Modern Art Bulletin*, New York, vol. 12, November, 1944, pp. 7-9.

Sweeney, J. J. "An Interview with Jacques Lipchitz," *Partisan Review*, vol. 12, no. 1, Winter 1945, pp. 83-89.

Cassou, Jean. "Lipchitz," *Horizon*, London, vol. 14, December, 1946, pp. 377-380.

Pach, Walter. "Lipchitz and the Modern Movement," *Magazine of Art*, Washington, D. C., vol. 39, December, 1946, pp. 354-359.

Raynal, Maurice. "La sculpture de Jacques Lipchitz," *Arts de France*, Paris, no. 6, 1946, pp. 43-50.

Raynal, Maurice. *Jacques Lipchitz*. Paris, Editions Jeanne Bucher, 1947.

"Lipchitz," *Current Biography*, 1948, vol. 9, New York, H. W. Wilson, 1949, pp. 378-380.

Faure, Elie. "Jacques Lipchitz et le cubisme," *Arts Plastiques*, Brussels, no. 2, 1950, pp. 117-122. (Article written 1932-33.)

Frost, Rosamund J. "Lipchitz Makes a Sculpture," *Art News*, New York, vol. 42, April, 1950, pp. 36-39, 63-64.

Ritchie, Andrew Carnduff. *Jacques Lipchitz, an Exhibition of his Sculpture and Drawings, 1914-1950*. Portland, Art Museum, 1950.

Ritchie, Andrew Carnduff. *Sculpture of the Twentieth Century*. New York, The Museum of Modern Art, 1953, pp. 32, 42-43, 178-181.

Greenberg, Clement. "Sculpture of Jacques Lipchitz," *Commentary*, vol. 18, September, 1954, pp. 257-259.

Hess, Thomas B. "Lipchitz: Space for Modern Sculpture," *Art News*, New York, vol. 53, Summer, 1954, pp. 34-37, 61-62.

Hope, Henry R. *The Sculpture of Jacques Lipchitz*. New York, The Museum of Modern Art, 1954 (Catalogue of the exhibition).

Larrea, Juan. "An Open Letter to Jacques Lipchitz," *College Art Journal*, New York, vol. 13, no. 4, Summer, 1954, pp. 251-288.

Giedion-Welcker, Carola. *Contemporary Sculpture*. New York, Wittenborn, 1955, pp. 50-57. (A revised and enlarged edition of *Modern Plastic Art*, 1937.)

Kramer, Hilton. "Month in Review," *Arts*, New York, vol. 31, March, 1957, pp. 46-47. (Review of exhibition at Fine Arts Associates.)

Munro, E. C. "Sculptor in the Foundry: Lipchitz at Work," *Art News*, New York, vol. 56, March, 1957, pp. 28-30, 61-62.

Rodman, Selden. *Conversations With Artists*. New York, Devin-Adair Co., 1957, pp. 130-136.

Elsen, Albert E. "The Humanism of Rodin and Lipchitz," *College Art Journal*, New York, vol. 17, no. 3, Spring, 1958, pp. 247-265.

Goldwater, Robert. *Jacques Lipchitz*. New York, Universe Books, 1959. (First issued in Dutch, 1954.)

Guéguen, Paul. "Le nouveau colloque avec Lipchitz" (with English summary), *XXe Siècle*, Paris, no. 21, December, 1959, supplement, pp. 27-31.

Hope, Henry R. "Un sculpteur d'hier et d'aujourd'hui," *L'Oeil*, Lausanne, no. 53, May, 1959, pp. 30-37.

Schneider, Pierre. "Lipchitz: Cubism. The School for Baroque," *Art News*, New York, vol. 58, October, 1959, p. 46.

Werner, Alfred. "Protean Jacques Lipchitz," *The Painter and Sculptor*, vol. 2, no. 4, Winter 1959-1960, pp. 11-17.

Hammacher, A. M. *Jacques Lipchitz*. New York, Harry N. Abrams, Inc., 1960.

The Lipchitz Collection. Museum of Primitive Art, New York, 1960.

"Jacques Lipchitz montre sa collection," *l'Oeil*, Lausanne, no. 66, June, 1960, pp. 46-53.

Jacques Lipchitz. A Retrospective Exhibition of Sculpture and Drawings. Washington, D.C., The Corcoran Gallery of Art, March 12-April 10, 1960; The Baltimore Museum of Art, April 26-May 29, 1960.

Maillard, Robert. *Dictionary of Modern Sculpture.* New York, Tudor Publishing Co., 1960.

Seuphor, Michel. *The Sculpture of This Century.* New York, Braziller, 1960.

Arnason, H. H. *Modern Sculpture from the Joseph H. Hirshhorn Collection,* New York, The Solomon R. Guggenheim Museum, 1961, pp. 58-59, 97, 220.

Fifty Years of Lipchitz Sculpture. New York, Otto Gerson Gallery, November 7-December 9, 1961; Cornell University, January 8-February 11, 1962.

Greenberg, Clement. *Art and Culture.* Critical Essays. Boston, Beacon Press, 1961. "Jacques Lipchitz," pp. 105-110.

Kuh, Katharine. "Conclusions from an Old Cubist" (Interview), *Art News,* New York, vol. 60, November, 1961, pp. 48-49.

Patai, Irene. *Encounters: The Life of Jacques Lipchitz.* New York, Funk and Wagnalls, 1961.

Current Biography, 1962, vol. 23, New York, H. W. Wilson Co., pp. 262-264.

Kuh, Katherine. *The Artist's Voice.* New York, Harper & Row, 1962, pp. 155-170.

Sawin, Martica. "Gonzalez and Lipchitz," *Arts,* New York, vol. 36, February, 1962, pp. 14-19.

Vollmer, H. *Allgemeines Lexikon der bildenden Künstler des XX. Jahrhunderts,* 5 vols. & suppl. Leipzig, 1953-62.

Jacques Lipchitz. 157 Small Bronze Sketches, 1914-1962. New York, Otto Gerson Gallery, April 16-May 11, 1963.

Jacques Lipchitz: A Retrospective Selected by the Artist. Los Angeles, U.C.L.A. Art Council, 1963.

Marchiori, Giuseppe. *Modern French Sculpture.* New York, Harry N. Abrams, 1963.

Nordland, Gerald. "Lipchitz: Lively Legend," *Artforum,* vol. 1, no. 12, June, 1963, pp. 38-40.

Jacques Lipchitz. Retrospective. Sculpture and Drawing. Boston University, March 15-April 16, 1965.

Van Bork, Bert. *Lipchitz. The Artist at Work.* New York, Crown, 1966. With critical evaluation by Alfred Werner.

Images of Italy. Lipchitz. New York, Marlborough-Gerson, April-May, 1966.

Arnason, H. H. *History of Modern Art.* New York, Harry N. Abrams, 1968.

Ashton, Dore. *Modern American Sculpture.* New York, Harry N. Abrams, 1968.

Craven, Wayne. *Sculpture in America.* New York, Crowell Co., 1968.

Encyclopedia of World Art, 15 vols. New York, 1959-1968.

Lipchitz: The Cubist Period, 1913-1930. New York, Marlborough-Gerson, 1968.

Hammacher, A. M. *The Evolution of Modern Sculpture. Tradition and Innovation.* New York, Harry N. Abrams, 1969.

PLATES

1. *HEAD 1914 8¹/₂″*

2. *FIGURE   1915   18³/₄″*

3. *SEATED WOMAN IN ARMCHAIR   1921   5³/₈″*

4. *REPENTANT MAGDALENE   1921   3¹/₄″*

5. *RECLINING WOMAN* *1921* *2³/₄″*

6. *RECLINING WOMAN*   *1921*   3¹/₄″

7. STUDY FOR GARDEN STATUE   1921   5³/₈"

8. *STUDY FOR GARDEN VASE* *1923* *12"*

9. *FIGURE WITH GUITAR* 1922 8½"

10. *RECLINING FIGURE WITH GUITAR   1923   7³/₄"*

11. *FIGURES WITH MUSICAL INSTRUMENTS   1923   **8"***

12. *FIGURES WITH MUSICAL INSTRUMENTS 1923 9^1/$_4$"*

13. *MUSICAL INSTRUMENTS—Bas-Relief 1923 9¹/₂"*

14. *STUDY FOR STANDING BAS-RELIEF   1923   8⁵/₈″*

15. *FIGURE WITH GUITAR* 1924 6"

16. *FIGURE WITH GUITAR   1925   9"*

17. *WOMAN WITH GUITAR* 1925 6¹/₂″

18. *WOMAN WITH GUITAR   1925   5¹/₂″*

19. *WOMAN WITH MANDOLIN   1925   5"*

20. *MEDITATION 1925 8¹/₄″*

21. *MAN LEANING ON HIS ELBOWS 1925 4¹/₂″*

22. *FIRST IDEA FOR SACRIFICE   1925   7¹/₄″*

23. *PLOUMANACH* *1926* *7"*

24. *STUDY FOR PLOUMANACH* *1926* 8³/₄″

25. FIGURE 1926 9³/₄"

26. MEDITATION   1926   7"

27. *STANDING FIGURE   1926   8"*

28. *RECLINING FIGURE   1928   5"*

29. *DANCER WITH VEIL* *1928* 13"

30. *RECLINING WOMAN WITH DRAPERY 1928 13³/4"*

31. *DANCER WITH VEIL*   *1928*   6¹/₂″

32. *BIRDS* *1928* 3¹/₂″

33. *STUDY FOR A MATZEVA   1928   8"*

34. *RECLINING WOMAN 1929 4¹/₄″*

35. *COUPLE IN HAMMOCK* *1929* 9¹/₂″

36. *RECLINING FIGURE   1929   6"*

37. *STANDING FIGURE   1929   8¹/₄″*

38. *WOMAN LEANING ON A COLUMN* *1929* *13"*

39. *WOMAN LEANING ON A COLUMN*   *1929*   9⁵/₈″

40. *WOMAN LEANING ON A COLUMN* *1929* 11³/₄″

41. *RECLINING WOMAN ON A PUFF* 1929 7"

42. *DANCER 1929* 3¹/₈″

43. *MOTHER AND CHILD 1929 4"*

44. *FORM SEEN IN A CLOUD*   *1929*   **9¹/₂″**

45. *ENCOUNTER* *1929* 9³/₄″

46. *THE COUPLE 1929* **4³/₄″**

47. *LEDA 1929 4"*

48. *MAN WITH A CLARINET* *1929* 6³/₈″

49. *RETURN OF THE PRODIGAL SON* *1930* **8¹/₈″**

50. *RETURN OF THE PRODIGAL SON*   *1930*   7³/₈″

51. *RETURN OF THE PRODIGAL SON   1930   8¹/₈″*

52. *FIGURE* *1930* **10"**

53. *SEATED WOMAN* *1930* 7¹/₂″

54. *SEATED WOMAN* *1930* 8³/₄″

55. *MOTHER AND CHILD   1930   5"*

56. *CINDERELLA   1930   5¹/₈″*

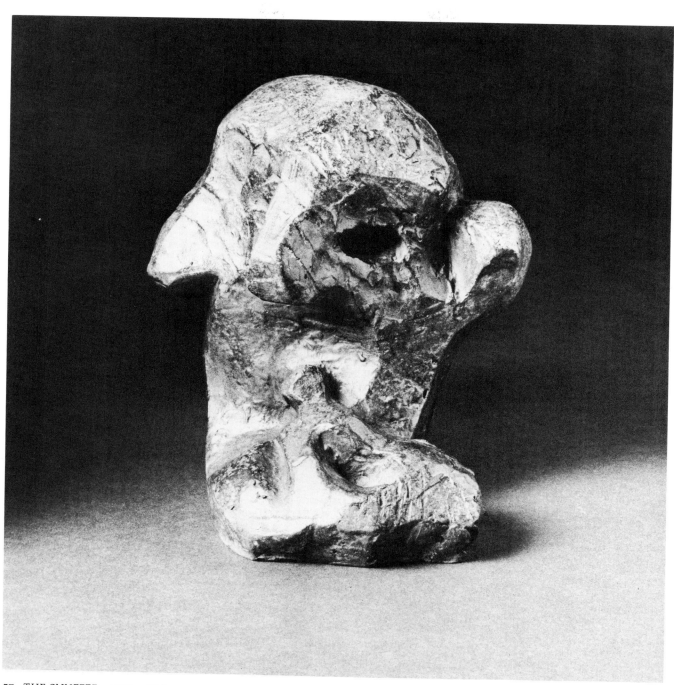

57. *THE SNUFFER   1930   6⁷/₈"*

58. *DESPERATION   1930   5"*

59. *MISHUGAS* 1930 8¹/₄"

60. *HEAD OF WOMAN   1930   6″*

61. *HEAD OF WOMAN AND HAIR AND HAND   1930   6"*

62. *WOMAN LEANING ON ELBOWS*   *1931*   *7³/₈″*

63. *MEDITATION* *1931* *7¹/₂″*

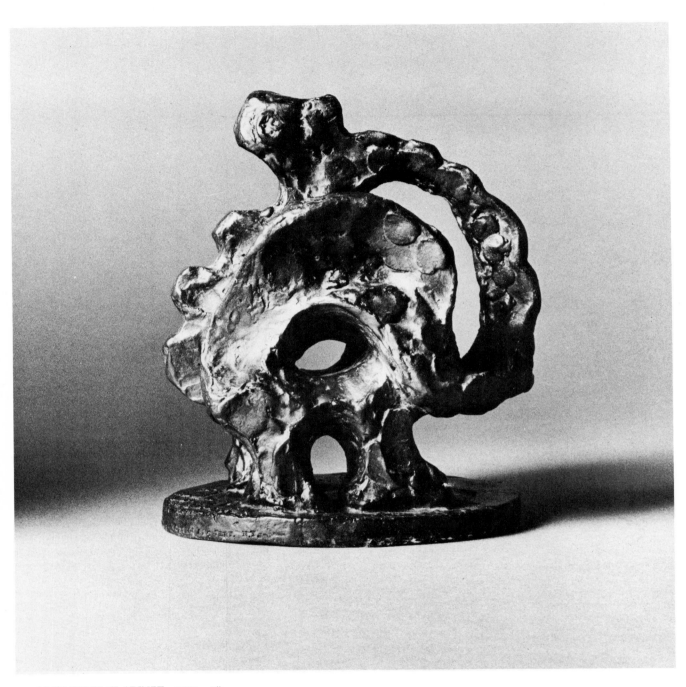

64. *MAN WITH CLARINET   1931   7"*

65. *THE FIGHT* *1931* *7³/₈″*

66. *JACOB AND THE ANGEL* *1931* 9¹/₄"

67. JACOB AND THE ANGEL   1931   8³/₄″

68. *FIRST STUDY FOR PROMETHEUS 1931 4¹/₂"*

69. *STUDY FOR "SONG OF THE VOWELS"* 1931 14³/₈"

70. *HEAD AND CROSSED ARMS* *1932* *5⅝″*

71. *HEAD AND HANDS* 1932 5¹/₂"

72. *HAIR AND HANDS*   *1932*   13¹/₈″

73. *LEANING ON HEAD AND HANDS*   *1932*   *5¹/₂"*

74. *HEAD AND HAND   1932   8″*

75. WOMAN LEANING ON HAND   1932   6"

76. *BUST OF A WOMAN* *1932* *7¹/₂″*

77. *WOMAN WITH HAIR* 1932 4"

78. *HEAD, BUST AND ARMS   1932   7¹/₄″*

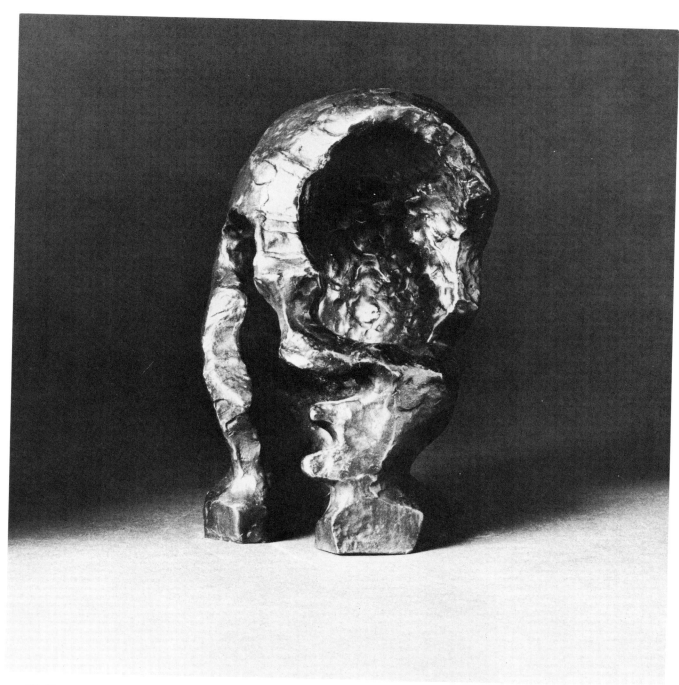

79. *HEAD* *1932* **8³/₄″**

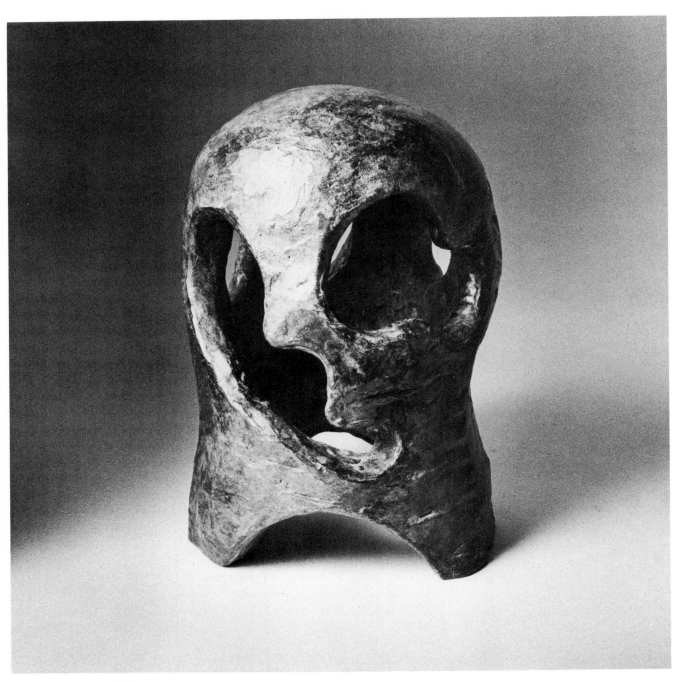

80. *HEAD* *1932* 8⁵/₈″

81. *BULL AND CONDOR*   *1932*   *7³/₄"*

82. *BULL AND CONDOR* *1932* *7⁷/₈"*

83. *WOMAN ON ELBOW 1933 9"*

84. *HEAD, HAIR AND HANDS   1933   6¹/₂"*

85. *LEANING ON HEAD AND HANDS   1933   8"*

86. *HEAD LEANING ON HANDS   1933   8¹/₂″*

87. *THE ARMS   1933   7"*

88. *BULL AND CONDOR*   *1933*   14$^1/_2$″

89. *RESCUE OF THE CHILD   1933   10¹/₄″*

90. *RESCUE OF THE CHILD   1933   12¹/₂"*

91. *RESCUE OF THE CHILD*　1933　10¹/₄″

92. *THE EMBRACE   1933   5″*

93. *THE EMBRACE* *1933* 6¹/₄″

94. *THE RAPE   1933   5¹/₈″*

95. *THE STRANGULATION 1933* 5³/₄″

96. *PROMETHEUS AND THE VULTURE* 1933 8¼"

97. *DAVID AND GOLIATH* *1933* **9¹/₂″**

98. *DAVID AND GOLIATH   1933   6¹/₄″*

99. DAVID AND GOLIATH   1933   10¹/₂"

100. *DAVID AND GOLIATH*   *1933*   12⁵/₈″

101. GERICAULT 1933 7¹/₄"

102. *GERICAULT* *1933* *9¹/₂"*

103. *HEAD OF GERICAULT* *1933* 7¹/₄"

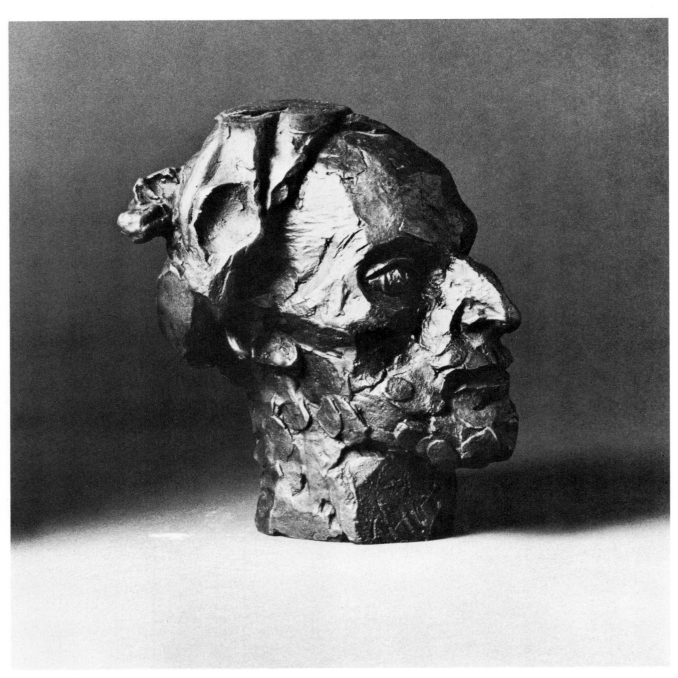

104. *GERICAULT   1933   8¹/₂″*

105. *FIRST STUDY FOR PASTORAL*   *1934*   4³/₄″

106. *THE LOVERS* *1934* 6³/₈″

107. *FIRST STUDY FOR "TOWARD A NEW WORLD"   1934   5"*

108. *TOWARD A NEW WORLD*   *1934*   7⁵/₈″

109. *TOWARD A NEW WORLD   1934   8³/₄″*

110. *TOWARD A NEW WORLD* *1934* 9⁵/₈″

111. *STUDY FOR A MONUMENT   1934   12"*

112. *STUDY FOR A MONUMENT*   *1934*   *13³/₈″*

113. *STUDY FOR A MONUMENT   1934   15"*

114. *STUDY FOR THE POTTER 1935 19³/₄″*

115. *STUDY FOR THE POTTER*   *1936*   **12⁵/₈"**

116. *STUDY FOR WALL DECORATION*   *1936*   12³/₄″

117. *THE TERRIFIED ONE*   *1936*   14³/₈″

118. *STUDY FOR A MONUMENT* *1936* *6⁷/₈″*

119. *STUDY FOR A BRIDGE MONUMENT* *1936* *15″*

120. *SCENE OF CIVIL WAR*   *1936*   9¹/₄″

121. *STUDY FOR PROMETHEUS* *1936* 10¹/₄″

122. *STUDY FOR PROMETHEUS   1936   7¹/₂″*

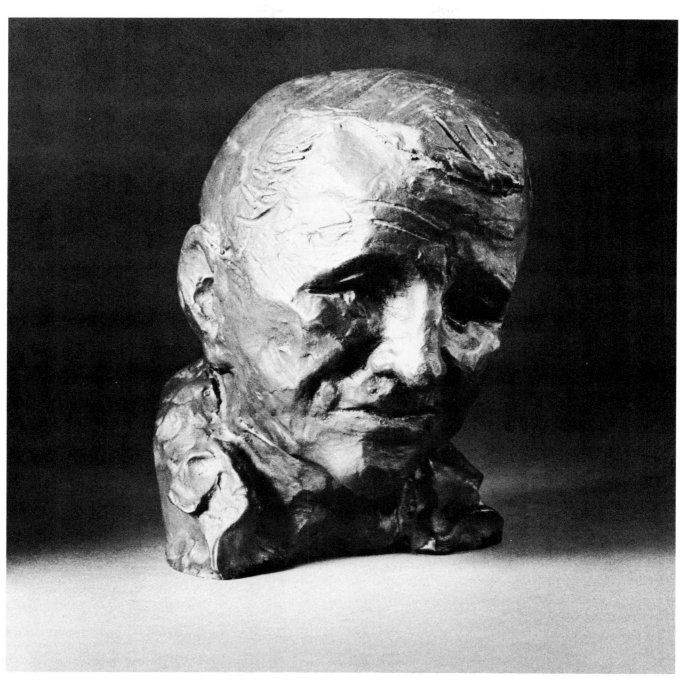

123. *SKETCH FOR GERTRUDE STEIN* 1938 7¹/₂"

124. *SKETCH OF GERTRUDE STEIN   1938   11¹/₂″*

125. *STUDY FOR "RETURN OF THE CHILD"*   *1941*   *11⁵/₈"*

126. *STUDY FOR BENEDICTION*   *1942*   6³/₈"

127. *STUDY FOR BENEDICTION* *1942* *7⁷/₈″*

128. *STUDY FOR BENEDICTION*   *1942*   14⁵/₈″

129. *PROMETHEUS STRANGLING THE VULTURE*   *1943*   *20¹/₂″*

130. *FIRST STUDY FOR "SONG OF SONGS"   1944   4⅝"*

131. *FIRST STUDY FOR "BIRTH OF THE MUSES"* 1944 5"

132. *MOTHER AND CHILD* *1945* **5³/₄"**

133. *THE COUPLE* *1947* **8"**

134. *THE COUPLE* *1947* *5"*

135. *DANCER* *1947* **8"**

136. *DANCER WITH VEIL* 1947 9¹/₂″

137. *STUDY FOR DANCER WITH BRAIDS*   *1947*   13⁵/₈″

138. *HAGAR   1948   5$^7/_8$"*

139. *HAPPINESS*   *1947*   9³/₈″

140. *STUDY FOR THE VIRGIN*   *1948*   9³/₄″

141. *STUDY FOR THE VIRGIN*   *1948*   8¼"

142. *STUDY FOR THE VIRGIN*   *1948*   8³/₄"

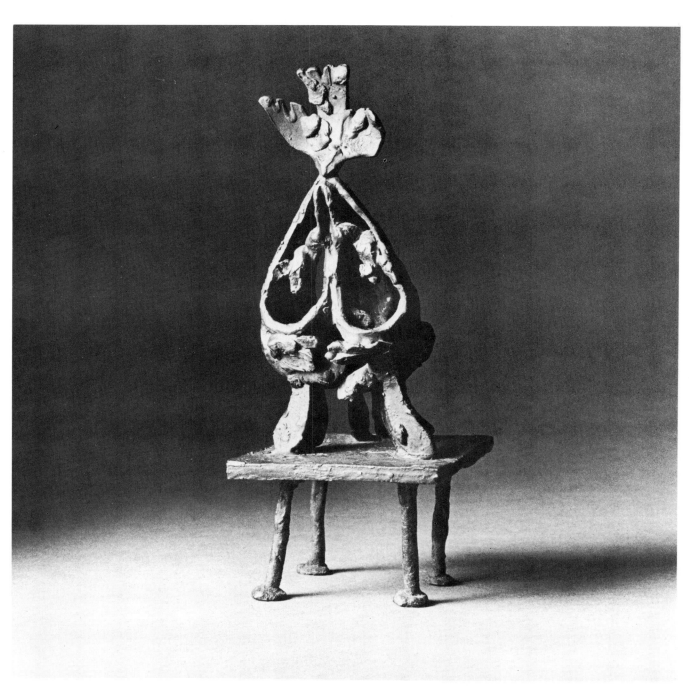

143. *STUDY FOR THE VIRGIN*   *1948*   10¹/₄″

144. *STUDY FOR THE VIRGIN   1949   9"*

145. *SKETCH FOR PEGASUS   1949   9¹/₈″*

146. *PEGASUS* *1949* 12⁵/₈″

147. *BIBLICAL SCENE*   *1949*   20¹/₄"

148. *STUDY FOR BIBLICAL SCENE   1949   12¹/₂″*

149. *SKETCH FOR ENTERPRISE   1953   11¹/₄″*

150. *SKETCH FOR ENTERPRISE   1953   9¹/₈″*

151. *SKETCH FOR ENTERPRISE* *1953* *16¹/₂″*

152. *STUDY FOR PORTRAIT   1956   13"*

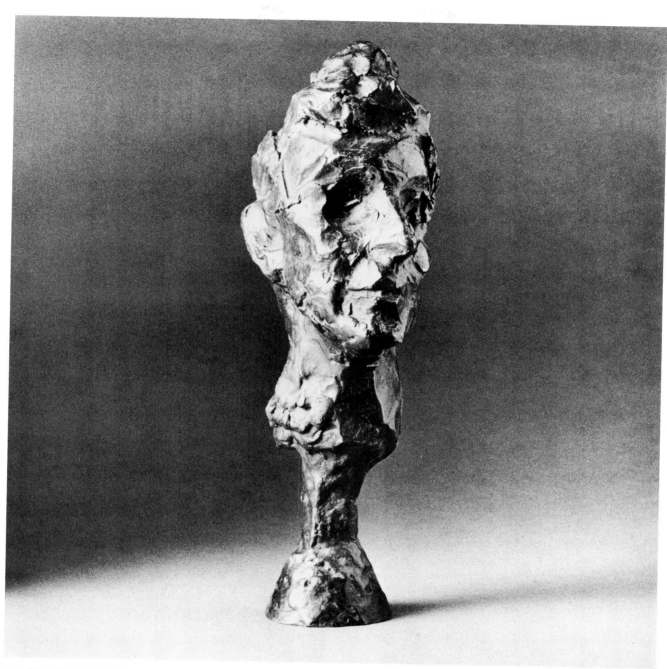

153. *SKETCH FOR YULLA LIPCHITZ* 1956 12¹/₈″

154. *LESSON OF A DISASTER   1956   10³/₈″*

155. *SKETCH FOR THE GATE OF THE ROOFLESS CHURCH* 1958 17¹/₈"

156. *STUDY FOR "OUR TREE OF LIFE"* *1962* 15¹/₂"

157. *SKETCH OF "OUR TREE OF LIFE"   1962   34"*

158. *SKETCH FOR JOHN F. KENNEDY   1964   18"*

159. *SKETCH FOR DANIEL GREYSOLON, SIEUR DU LUTH   1962   23″*

160. *STUDY FOR DULUTH MONUMENT   1963   26"*

161. BELLEROPHON TAMING PEGASUS   1964   20″